W

When Summer Comes

Helen Naylor

CAMBRIDGE
UNIVERSITY PRESS

PUBLISHED BY THE PRESS SYNDICATE OF THE UNIVERSITY OF CAMBRIDGE
The Pitt Building, Trumpington Street, Cambridge, United Kingdom

CAMBRIDGE UNIVERSITY PRESS
The Edinburgh Building, Cambridge CB2 2RU, UK
40 West 20th Street, New York, NY 10011-4211, USA
477 Williamstown Road, Port Melbourne, VIC 3207, Australia
Ruiz de Alarcón 13, 28014 Madrid, Spain
Dock House, The Waterfront, Cape Town 8001, South Africa

http://www.cambridge.org

First published 2001
Seventh printing 2004

Printed in India by Thomson Press

Typeset in 12/15pt Adobe Garamond [CE]

ISBN 0 521 65611 7

Contents

Characters

Anna Martins: aged thirty. A nurse. Lives in London. Married to Stephen for ten years.

Stephen Martins: aged thirty-two. Works for an advertising agency. Lives in London. Married to Anna for ten years.

Tristan Goddard: early thirties. Lives and works in Polreath as a fisherman. Runs boat trips for visitors in the summer. The owner of Dolphin Cottage.

Jill: Tristan's girlfriend. Used to live in Polreath, now lives in London.

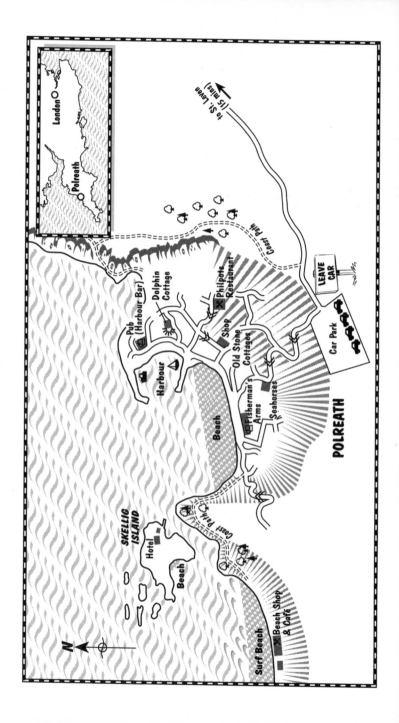

Chapter 1   *The city heat*

'When we get to Polreath on Saturday, I'm going to do nothing,' said Anna. 'I just want to sit and have cool drinks and read and watch the world go by.'

'Me too,' replied Stephen.

It was the hottest summer for twenty years. It had started at the end of May. Everyone thought the heat would only last for a few days and then the rain would return, but this summer was different.

'And don't expect any intelligent conversation from me,' Anna continued. 'It'll take a day or two for me to become a member of the human race again!'

'Mm,' said Stephen, not really listening. 'What about this cottage we've booked, do you think it's going to be all right? To be honest, I'm a bit worried about it – we were so late making our decision and it was still available. Why didn't anyone else want it? It makes me think there must be something wrong with it.'

'Don't worry. I'm sure it'll be fine. And even if it's not, we'll still be away from here. Just think – three weeks by the sea, without any work. It sounds wonderful.'

In the city the heat was uncomfortable. People were not used to high temperatures day after day. Journeys to work became hot and sweaty, and increasingly bad-tempered in the crowded trains and buses. By the beginning of July, nobody could remember when it had last rained. Everywhere you looked seemed to be brown – the grass in the parks was burnt and most of the flowers had died. The sun was burning hot and the air seemed to be getting thicker and thicker. At the weekends, the place was empty as many people left for the countryside.

But Stephen and Anna couldn't leave – not until the weekend anyway.

*   *   *

Stephen was thirty-two with dark, curly hair. He had noticed a few grey hairs that morning when he was drying it after his shower. But he didn't mind too much; in fact, he rather liked the idea of a few which might make him look serious. But his face showed signs of stress and worry.

Stephen left the flat just before seven. He was earlier than usual this morning because he wanted to avoid the rush hour, but it seemed as if everyone else had had the same idea – the roads were busy and there had been an accident half way along Sussex Gardens. He waited impatiently while the police sorted out the chaos but by the time he arrived at work, he was late and not in a very good mood.

He locked the Saab and went into the cool building. The offices of Jardine and Makepeace, advertising agents, were on the fourteenth floor of a modern block with wonderful views over Regent's Park. But this morning, when Stephen found himself climbing the stairs (the lift was out of order again!), he would happily have given up the views for an office on the ground floor.

'Please let everything go smoothly today,' he said to himself as he made his way up the stairs.

Stephen was worried about work – the agency had lost an important client that week. He felt that Charlie Jardine, the agency boss, blamed him. A couple of days before, he'd passed by Charlie's office and had heard him saying on the phone, 'Yes, well, I'll have to talk to Stephen about that. He was the one working on their new advertisement.' Stephen hadn't heard any more but he thought that Charlie sounded a bit angry.

He wondered if it was a bad time to go on holiday – perhaps his job would disappear when he was away. But he didn't want to miss this break – and in any case, Anna would kill him if he suggested cancelling. So he said nothing to her about his worries. He often found it hard to talk about his problems, even with Anna. God knows why, she was usually willing to listen.

In his mind, he would think through different ways of opening the conversation with her, but everything he thought of sounded so obvious – 'I'm worried about work' or 'I'd like to talk to you about something'. In any case, he really preferred to work things out himself. But he knew he was not easy to live with when he didn't talk much.

'Morning Mark. Another lovely day,' panted Stephen, and sat down to get his breath back. His shirt was wet and sticking to his back.

'Morning Stephen,' said Mark. 'I'm not sure if it is a lovely day. Clare's away – she's got food poisoning or something – so between us we've got to do her work as well as our own.'

'Oh hell! Just what I needed to hear!' replied Stephen.

Anna's last day began even earlier. At 6.30 that morning she yawned as she walked across to St Phillips Hospital. It was another beautiful morning – for her the best time of the day when the air was still fresh and the day was still full of promise.

Her nurse's cap sat comfortably on her short blond hair. She looked fresh and efficient in her blue uniform. She loved her job as a nurse but it was hard. There always seemed to be so much to do – more than ever since the new manager had arrived.

'This weekend, when we're away,' she thought, 'I'm going to get up early and walk along the beach before anyone else is awake.' Then she laughed at the idea of getting up early when she didn't have to! Well, maybe she would – who knows, holidays can change people. Maybe that's what she needed – change. She was thirty and had been working at St Phillips since she'd finished her training – perhaps it was time to move on.

Later in the day she went to say goodbye to Michael Barton, a favourite patient who was recovering from a major operation.

'Have a wonderful holiday!' he said.

'Thanks, I will. And I hope I won't see you when I get back,' replied Anna. And as soon as she said it, she realised what a stupid thing it was to say.

'I mean, I hope you won't still be in hospital, you know, you'll be back at home,' she said quickly.

'It's all right, love. I know you weren't talking about me dying! I hope I don't see you either – although I'll miss you looking after me. Bye – all the best.'

She left the ward knowing that this time tomorrow she would be in a different world. She got off the hospital bus at the end of her street and walked slowly home, thinking about a cool beer in the back garden. They were lucky. Their flat was on the ground floor of a nineteenth-century house and the garden at the back was theirs. The garden wasn't big but it was a wonderful place to escape to in the summer. She wondered what sort of day Stephen had had. She knew something was worrying him but was too tired to do anything about it. Anyway, she knew from past experience that it was no use asking directly. He'd once told her that he could only talk about difficult things after they were past and no longer difficult. 'I'll find out what it is on holiday,' she thought. 'When we've got more time and energy.'

As Stephen was about to leave the office that evening, Charlie Jardine called him into his office and told him that there were going to be some changes in the next month, that probably one member of staff would have to go – 'be made redundant' was how Charlie said it, but Stephen thought 'sacked ... fired ... dismissed' was what he really wanted to say. Then Charlie said, 'But of course, I don't want to lose you.' Why didn't that make Stephen feel better? He left work with a heavy heart.

Chapter 2   *On the way*

'Got everything?' asked Anna.

'I don't care if we haven't!' said Stephen. 'Let's go! You drive.'

'OK. We've got to stop at Rebecca's to leave our keys with her,' said Anna, shutting the front door quietly behind her. 'She said she'd come in and make sure everything is OK while we're away. Remember? Oh, and did you write down our holiday address for her – she said she wanted it in case of emergencies. Though I don't think I want to know if there *are* any emergencies, do you? Now where did I put the car keys?'

'You always think you've lost the keys, and you never have,' said Stephen. 'I think you just say it to annoy me. Get in and drive! I've got the address for Rebecca, I've got the map, I've got the address of the cottage and you've got enough bottles of suntan cream to protect an army. Now, come on! We're wasting valuable holiday time!'

'Right. I'll drive first. Why don't you go to sleep? I'll wake you when it's your turn to drive,' said Anna.

London looked a bit like a ghost town at seven o'clock that Saturday morning. Either everybody had left it for their own holidays or they were still in bed. It was good to leave the city behind as Anna set off west along the M4 on the 500 kilometre drive to Polreath. Polreath was a small, quiet fishing village on the north-west coast of Cornwall with a few holiday cottages, two hotels, and the usual shops, bars and restaurants. It was famous for its seafood restaurants – lobsters, prawns, crabs – and relatively unspoilt – a great place to relax.

It would take most of the day to get there but Anna was happy to drive. It gave her time to think about last night when Stephen had come home from work. He had looked almost ill – he said it was only the heat and the traffic, and he just needed some peace and quiet. He had gone into the garden with a bottle of beer and walked around looking as if he was interested in the flowers (which she knew he wasn't). She had left him alone and after a while he came in for dinner, seeming a bit more cheerful. They had had a perfectly pleasant evening talking about arrangements for the next day and had gone to bed without mentioning work. But later, she had woken up and heard him in the kitchen, talking to someone on the telephone. When he had come back to bed, she had pretended to be asleep. In the morning, neither of them had mentioned it. 'Oh well, when we've both relaxed, perhaps he'll talk about it,' thought Anna.

The sun was behind her and she could feel its warmth on her shoulders. There wasn't much traffic about so she put her foot down, and as the kilometres passed, she felt her head begin to clear of all the worries, the questions. She put a cassette on quietly – a little Mozart for company, perfect – and started to enjoy the drive.

'Where are we?' asked Stephen sleepily.

'We've just passed Bristol, so I suppose we're doing well,' said Anna. 'Your turn to drive.'

'OK. Let's stop and have a cup of coffee first.'

Anna turned into the next service area where they had to queue for a fairly awful cup of coffee. Half an hour later they were back on the road, this time with Stephen driving. He changed the music to an Ella Fitzgerald tape and Anna attempted to sing along with her.

'I think I prefer Ella Fitzgerald to you, if you don't mind,' joked Stephen.

'Sorry, this song always makes me want to sing,' replied Anna. 'Don't worry, I'll go to sleep in a minute.'

Stephen turned off the motorway. He reckoned it would take about another three hours to get to Polreath. Anna was asleep. 'She wasn't last night, though, when I came back to bed after that phone call, I know. She's not very good at pretending.' Stephen looked at her lovingly. 'Perhaps it was a mistake to ring Mark, but I wanted to tell him what Charlie had said about making someone redundant. Now all I've done is make Mark feel bad, too. I must be going mad. Why did I tell him? He'll find out soon enough if he's going to lose his job.'

Anna moved beside him.

'Not long now,' said Stephen, trying to forget about work. 'I'll be really happy to get out of this hot car, won't you?'

'Mmm.'

'First thing I'm going to do is have a swim,' he said.

'What about unpacking the car, and buying a few things like milk and bread for tomorrow's breakfast?' said Anna.

'To hell with that. We're on holiday and we're going to do what we want to do, not what we should. No more planning, no more thinking ahead, no more worrying.'

'I'll remember you said that. This sounds as if it's going to be an interesting three weeks.'

Chapter 3   *Polreath*

Their first view of Polreath was from the top of a hill.

'Oh look, Stephen! The sea! And lots of little boats. It looks wonderful,' said Anna.

There was a big sign at the side of the road telling motorists not to drive into the village, that they must leave their cars in the car park.

'Right. Let's leave everything here. I'm going for a swim,' said Stephen.

'Me too,' replied Anna.

They walked hand in hand down the steep, narrow street to the beach below. The water wasn't wonderfully warm – this was the Atlantic after all – but even so that first swim was almost magical. Stephen lay on his back, looking at the sky and enjoying the first taste of freedom. Anna had swum quite a long way out but was now coming up towards him.

He turned towards her and they managed a salty kiss.

'Hello, love. Welcome to our new world,' said Anna softly.

'Hi, little one,' he said.

'You look ten years younger already. And that's after only one swim!'

They kissed again.

'Come on,' said Stephen, 'that's enough for now.'

'What, swimming or kissing?' asked Anna.

'Both,' he smiled, and kissed her again.

They swam slowly back to the beach. The sun still felt warm, so they sat on the sand for a few minutes with their towels wrapped round them. Outside a pub people were sitting with drinks and watching them in a leisurely way. Anna and Stephen – the only ones on the beach at that time suddenly realised that everyone's eyes were on them, so they picked up their things and left.

'We'd better go and introduce ourselves to Mr Goddard and get the key for the cottage,' Stephen said. 'He said to come to his house. What was it called, Anna?'

'Seahorses,' she replied. 'We passed it on the way down the hill. Look, you go. I want to change my clothes.

'I don't know, one look at you in your swimsuit and he might put the price down,' he replied.

'Very funny! I'll wait on the corner over there,' she said, giving him a little push.

Anna watched as Stephen knocked on the door of Seahorses. A youngish man appeared and she could hear Stephen introduce himself.

'Mr Goddard? Hello, I'm Stephen Martins. Sorry about my appearance but we got so hot travelling down here that we had to have a quick swim,' he said.

'No problem. I'm pleased you've arrived. I'm Tristan Goddard. Welcome.'

He looked over Stephen's shoulder and saw Anna standing at the corner. She gave a small wave and smiled.

'That's Anna,' said Stephen. 'She said she'd come and introduce herself when she's changed.'

'Fine. Well look, this is the key for Dolphin Cottage. Go down to the harbour, turn right and follow that little road until you come to a stone cottage. You can't miss it, it's the only one with a green door.'

'Thanks. By the way, what about cars in the village?' Stephen asked. 'Can I bring the car down? It's in the car park at the top of the hill at the moment.'

'Yeah,' replied Tristan. 'You can bring it down to unpack everything, but then you'll have to take it back up to the car park. We're trying to keep the village free of cars as much as possible. It used to be a real problem with the fishermen trying to get up and down to the harbour in their vans, and visitors parking on the streets. So now no visitors' cars are allowed. Sorry.'

'That's OK,' Stephen said, 'I'll be perfectly happy without it.'

'Fine. I'll come down a bit later then to see that everything's OK,' said Tristan.

Tristan stood on the step and watched Stephen join Anna. As they walked down the street holding hands, he couldn't help noticing how good she looked in her swim suit. They seemed very comfortable with each other, he thought, and wondered how long they'd been together. Half-smiling, he turned and went back into the house, with the picture of Stephen and Anna still in his head. Then the picture changed to him and Jill last summer when they'd been so happy. Now she was in London and God knows when they were going to be together again, if ever. She refused to live in Polreath – she said it was 'too dead in the winter', and he knew he couldn't live in London. In fact, he had no wish to live anywhere but Polreath. To him it had everything. For seven months of the year, the visitors brought life and work to the village and for the remaining five months the locals had the place to themselves. He loved it in the middle of winter when the sea was rough and the waves crashed over the harbour wall. It was impossible then for any of the fishermen to go to sea. And the village had the feeling of being an island with no way of escape.

Jill had wanted to leave as soon as the summer had finished, to go back to the bright lights. This summer, she'd been down and for a few weeks they'd got on as well together as last year. But soon he had seen that she was getting bored. And then the telephone call with the promise of a new, exciting job had pulled her back to London. They still spoke on the phone, but in his heart he knew that the whole thing was over.

He sighed sadly and sat down to plan his work for tomorrow. During the summer months he took visitors in his boat to Skellig – the island off the headland – on fishing trips and on day-long trips along the coast, and anything else they wanted to do. And he still managed to do a bit of fishing between trips. His first trip was at 9.30 – ten people to take to Skellig.

He left the front door open to get a bit more air into the house and walked down the narrow streets to Dolphin Cottage.

'Hello, anyone at home?' called Tristan.

'Oh hello. I'm Anna. Come in.'

Anna led the way into the kitchen. Tristan followed and thought she looked good in jeans, too. Stephen was putting things away in cupboards.

'Is everything OK? Have you found your way around?' asked Tristan.

Stephen smiled, 'Yes, everything's just perfect. And thank you for buying the bread and milk and things. How much do we owe you for that?'

'Don't worry about it now, you can pay me at the end. I thought you might arrive after the shop had closed so I just bought a few essentials.'

'Thanks a lot,' said Anna.

Stephen had told Anna that Tristan seemed 'very nice', and she had to agree. She found herself almost staring at him. He had the most amazing eyes – sort of strong blue – that seemed to look through you. She thought he must be in his early thirties, about the same age as Stephen, but taller and slimmer, and with those wonderful eyes! He was saying something to Stephen but she wasn't really listening.

'What do you think, Anna? Shall we go?' said Stephen.

'What? Sorry, I wasn't listening. Shall we go where?'

'Tristan was just saying that he was running a boat trip to a little island at half past nine tomorrow morning and would we like to go?' said Stephen.

Anna said, 'Really? Do you often do boat trips?'

'Yes, there's something happening every day. In fact, you should find a list of trips on the wall by the back door.' Tristan pointed, 'Yes, look, there it is.'

She made herself turn round to look.

'I'd really quite like to explore Polreath tomorrow morning,' Anna said. 'It seems funny to go on a trip before we've had a look round here first. We can go on the boat any day.'

'True. We'll do that then, Tristan,' said Stephen. 'Have a day wandering around the village and then come with you later in the week.'

'OK. Well, I'll be off now and leave you to it,' Tristan said, moving towards the door. 'If you've got any problems, you know where I live. Bye for now.'

Half an hour later, Stephen and Anna were sitting outside drinking coffee in the front garden. The cottage was exactly how they'd imagined it – a traditional fisherman's cottage built of stone with very thick walls to keep out the wind. The tiny garden at the front looked over the harbour.

'I can't believe our luck. Can you imagine anything more ideal than this?' asked Anna. 'And what about Tristan? Don't you think he's got the most amazing eyes. I couldn't stop looking at him.'

'I noticed! Actually, you're right, his eyes *are* interesting. I'd like eyes like that.'

'So would I. And I wouldn't mind his hair either. It's all curly like yours is when you've just had a shower, except his is really blond.'

'OK, that's enough about Tristan,' laughed Stephen. 'I might get jealous. Anyway, he can't be so good-looking *and* a really nice person – there's probably *something* wrong with him!'

Later, Stephen came into the bedroom drying his hair after a cool shower. Anna looked at him and smiled. She wondered if he remembered the conversation about Tristan's hair. Had he come in with wet hair deliberately, just to remind her that she'd always liked *his* hair?

They lay there, side by side, touching, with the sound of the sea coming through the open window.

Chapter 4 *Exploring the village*

The next day, Anna woke up not long after dawn. She could hear seagulls crying. She thought about an early morning walk. Maybe tomorrow, she decided, and turned over for a bit more sleep. She didn't notice that Stephen wasn't lying beside her.

Stephen had woken up even earlier and had heard the sounds of the birds. He lay there for a time, listening, but slowly his mind started to fill up with memories of his last conversation with his boss. 'Oh no,' he thought, 'I don't want to start thinking about that now. I'm on holiday, I need a break.' But the problems of the last few weeks at work wouldn't go away. He could feel his stomach begin to get tight – a sure sign that he was getting worried. 'It's no good,' he thought, 'I'll have to get up and do something.'

Quietly, he got dressed and left the cottage. The sun had just risen and the air already felt warm. He started jogging up the hill out of the village, hoping that some physical activity would help. By the time he reached the top he was a bit out of breath. He looked into the car park to make sure the car was still there, then carried on walking. There was a signpost saying "Footpath" so he went along it. It led to the edge of the cliff. At this point he was standing about a hundred metres above the sea, looking back down onto Polreath harbour. It was a wonderful view – one he felt he'd always remember. There were one or two people on their boats in the harbour, including a blond-haired man. 'I wonder if that's Tristan,' thought Stephen. He watched the activity in the harbour and slowly the tightness in his stomach started to go away. He felt calmer. He realised that the problems at work were not going to disappear; he was going to have to think about his job clearly and carefully, and decide what he really wanted to do. And try and talk to Anna about it. Once or twice recently he had seen her looking at him almost angrily. 'Poor Anna,' he thought. 'She must get fed up with me sometimes.'

He had started to walk back along the path when he heard voices from the harbour below. He turned and saw a dark-haired man standing at the front of a fishing boat, shouting at the blond man. They seemed to be having some sort of argument. The dark-haired man kept pointing at the blond man's boat. Stephen enjoyed the fact that other people seemed to have problems at work, too, not just him! And he watched as the two small boats left the harbour.

When he got back to Dolphin Cottage with some fresh bread, Anna was sitting in the front garden with a cup of coffee. She looked at him closely and said,

'Hello, are you all right?'

'Yes, I'm fine. I woke up early and decided to get some exercise ... and some fresh bread. Here, smell it, straight from the baker's.'

'Mm, delicious. Let's have breakfast out here. You can tell me what the village is like.'

Stephen told her about the argument in the harbour, and how he was sure one of the men was Tristan, but he didn't tell her what had made him get up so early. Time to get serious later, not now.

Stephen and Anna spent the rest of the morning wandering round the village. They walked up and down the narrow streets and paths, looking at everything. Most of the houses near the harbour were like theirs – old stone cottages. There were one or two which were obviously holiday cottages but most of them still seemed to be lived in by local people. A bit further away from the harbour, it seemed to be more mixed – some more modern houses and one or two very fine ones which had probably been built when it had first become fashionable for city people to take their holidays by the sea.

In one of the small side-streets, they found Philpots, a restaurant specialising in seafood. The menu promised lobster, crab and fish, all freshly caught.

'This looks wonderful.'

'And look at the prices! This lot would cost twice as much in London.'

Stephen felt a hand on his shoulder.

'Morning.' Tristan was standing behind them in shorts and a T-shirt. 'You were up early today, Stephen. I saw you leaving the cottage.'

'Yes, I went jogging,' replied Stephen. 'I didn't see you, though.'

'I was on the boat – just going out for an hour or two's fishing,' said Tristan.

'Ah, so it was him,' thought Stephen. 'Did you catch anything?' he asked Tristan.

'I just put down the lobster pots. I'll go back later and pull them up. I usually get a few and then sell them to this place. So if you eat here tonight, they might be serving my lobsters,' said Tristan, looking at Anna.

'Great,' said Anna. 'How was the trip to the island?'

'Oh fine. I left the people there for the day. There's not much to do, but that's what's attractive, I suppose. They just walk round, look at the few people who actually live there and think how wonderful it'd be to have a house on a small island. They see it on a wonderful, sunny day like today and don't think about the times in the winter when it's cut off for days by the storms. But it's a very special place and you need to be a special kind of person to be able to enjoy it!'

For some reason, Stephen felt Tristan was that special kind of person – a man who would be happy with his own company.

'Well, see you later. Have a good day,' said Tristan, and walked off in the direction of the harbour.

'Let's go and have lunch in that pub by the beach, and plan the rest of the day,' said Anna.

'OK,' replied Stephen. 'Well, we now know two things about Tristan. One, not everybody here likes him – remember I told you about that argument in the harbour this morning – and two, he seems to have strong feelings about the island.'

'And three, he's got nice legs!' said Anna as she watched him climb onto his boat.

'Anna! Can't you think of anything except his eyes and legs? Honestly! And they say it's men who think about sex all the time!' Stephen's voice sounded half-serious. Actually, he was a bit surprised. He'd never known Anna talk so openly about a man's physical appearance. He didn't quite know whether to be worried about it.

'It's all right. I'm only joking. I'm sure he's a very interesting person . . . as well as good to look at!'

At the Fisherman's Arms they had crab salads and ice-cold beer. They sat outside in friendly silence and watched the activity on the beach.

'Shall we walk over in that direction this afternoon?' Stephen pointed to the left. 'We could go along the coast path – see what there is over the hill.'

'OK, but let's not hurry off just yet,' said Anna.

They got some more drinks. Anna stretched out her long legs in the sun and started to read the guide book for the area. Stephen watched her while drinking his beer. Everything about her seemed so familiar. 'She looks so happy sitting there, like a cat in the sun,' he thought. 'She's got a lovely face, so full of life and smiles – except when I worry her with my silences.' He suddenly heard a loud voice behind him.

'Bloody Tristan,' said a man at another table. 'He thinks he owns the village. Why does he want to buy another house? He's already got two. How many more does he want?'

'Ssh. Not so loud, Jack. In any case, you don't know if he does yet,' said the man sitting with him in a low voice.

'Well, you heard him asking about how much the cottage was being sold for. He wants it, I'm sure,' said Jack. 'Then he'll rent it out as a holiday place, just like he's done with Dolphin Cottage.'

Anna and Stephen sat there, pretending not to listen.

'Come on, he's got to rent Dolphin Cottage out, he can't live in two places at once, can he? In any case, that woman, what's her name, Jane ... Jill, has been living there,' the other man said.

'Well, she doesn't live there now, does she?' replied Jack. 'I don't know, he talks a lot about trying to keep the village the same – "unspoilt", that's what he says – but if you ask me, it'll be ruined in a few years' time.'

'This place has stood here for a few hundred years, I'm sure it'll go on a bit longer. Anyway, I don't believe Tristan'll buy another cottage – why should he?'

'I asked him this morning, and he didn't say no,' Jack answered.

'Knowing you, you probably didn't give him time to answer your question before you got angry with him,' the other man replied.

The man called Jack left the pub, still complaining about 'bloody Tristan'. The other man stayed at the bar, staring into his beer.

'Help!' whispered Anna. 'I'm glad he didn't realise *we* were the people renting Dolphin Cottage.'

'Come on,' said Stephen, standing up. 'Let's go for our walk.' They walked out of the village along the coast path. Although they talked about what they'd heard in the bar, they were not really worried – just interested in the life of the village and what part Tristan Goddard played in it. They knew that over the next three weeks they'd probably discover what it was all about.

They followed the path through some trees, happy to escape from the hot sun for a while. Eventually, they walked round a corner and came to a wide bay with people surfing on beautiful, white waves.

'Hey, that looks fun,' said Stephen. 'I've always wanted to try it.'

'I did it once when I was about fifteen,' said Anna. 'I wasn't very good at it. Every time I stood up, I fell off. But I'll have another go. Age might have improved my balance.'

A woman in the beach shop told them they could hire surf boards there and, if they wanted, they could also have lessons.

'Right. So, there's no reason why we shouldn't try, then. Thanks for the information. We'll be back another day,' Stephen smiled.

They walked slowly back towards Polreath, changed into their swimming things at the cottage and went down to the beach. The sand was warm from the day's sun and Stephen fell asleep lying there. Anna continued reading her local guide book. This was always the first thing she bought when she went to a new place, and a map of the area. She enjoyed getting information which she'd then pass on to Stephen – who, actually, didn't always want to know! In fact, she sometimes annoyed him with her facts.

Stephen woke up, saw Anna with her nose in the book and knew that tonight in the restaurant she was going to say, 'I read in the guide book that ...' many times! He turned over quietly and ran his finger down her back.

'Oh, hello! Had a good sleep? You probably needed it after your early start this morning.'

'Mmm.' He stood up and stretched. 'Time for a swim?'

'Why not,' she replied. 'Then I'm going home for a quick sleep before dinner.'

Chapter 5 *Philpots*

Sitting at dinner in Philpots that evening, Anna felt wonderful. The fresh air, the sun, the swimming, everything had made her feel so alive. She found it hard to remember the Anna of a few days ago, and she almost couldn't recognise Stephen he looked so relaxed.

'You've got a red nose,' she said.

'It's not red, it's the light in this restaurant. And have you seen yours, by the way?'

'Yes, it looks very healthy,' she replied.

'Why is mine red and yours healthy?' he laughed.

'What are you having?' she asked, changing the subject.

'Need you ask?' said Stephen. 'Lobster à l'Américaine, of course. And you?'

'The same. Do you think it's one of Tristan's?'

'Will we be able to taste the difference?' he joked.

Anna knew that over dinner Stephen would probably find it easy to start talking about the things that were making him unhappy, but she didn't want him to. She wanted a relaxed, uncomplicated meal – an evening without thinking about London, work or Stephen's problems. So she deliberately kept the conversation away from anything serious.

'Hey, look at that! Doesn't it look wonderful,' Anna said when the waiter brought their plates to the table. The warm lobster pieces covered each plate, and a little bowl of extra sauce came with it. She dipped some bread into the sauce, 'This is seriously delicious!'

The lobster was followed by a lime and lemon dessert, and a wonderful selection of cheeses. They finished with strong coffee.

'We're going to be all right here, aren't we?' said Anna as they stood up to go. 'I think this is going to turn out to be our best holiday ever.'

'I hope so,' said Stephen.

Just as they were leaving, Tristan arrived.

'Evening. I thought you might be here,' he said. 'I just wondered if you'd like to come fishing tomorrow morning Stephen? You obviously get up early and I usually go out about six, six thirty for a couple of hours. You too, Anna, if you'd like.'

'Thanks, Tristan,' said Stephen, 'I'd enjoy that. What about you, Anna?'

'I'd rather have a bit longer in bed tomorrow morning. I'm still catching up on my sleep. But you go, Stephen.'

'Meet me at the harbour at about six tomorrow then,' said Tristan. 'It's a blue boat called Wave Dancer.'

'Right. See you there, and thanks again. Goodnight.'

'That should be interesting,' said Anna to Stephen as they walked home. 'I shall expect you to find out every-thing about him – all that business with that man in the pub yesterday, who the woman is who lived in our cottage – everything, please.'

'I'm going fishing, I'm not going to question him about his private life!' Stephen laughed. 'If I catch anything we can have it for tomorrow night's dinner, can't we?'

'Yes, but don't bring home a lobster, please. I don't know

whether I could cook one of those. They're alive when you put them in boiling water and they make a terrible noise. I know it's stupid but I'd rather eat lobster at Philpots and not hear them dying.'

'Don't worry,' Stephen said. 'I don't expect Tristan will let me have one. I should think he needs to sell the expensive stuff to make some money.'

* * *

At six the next morning, Tristan was waiting on his boat, Wave Dancer. He was dressed in the shorts he seemed to live in during the hot weather. He was wondering why he'd asked Stephen and Anna to come with him. He didn't usually ask the Dolphin Cottage people out on his boat in his 'private' time, but there was something he liked about Stephen and Anna – they were different. But was he feeling just the smallest bit of disappointment that it was only Stephen who was coming?

He turned and looked up at Dolphin Cottage, just in time to see Stephen coming out, pulling a black T-shirt over his head. A few minutes later, he jumped onto the boat.

'Am I late? Sorry,' he said. 'Had a bit of difficulty waking up this morning. Could be something to do with the excellent wine last night!'

Tristan smiled. 'Do you know anything about boats?' he asked.

'Sure. I'm used to boats. We always had holidays by the sea when I was a kid, and my parents taught me what to do.'

They left the harbour and turned north following the coast. Tristan dropped some lobster pots into the sea and said he'd collect them later that day. The sea was calm as they continued northwards. It was a bit cooler on the water than on the land and Stephen was pleased he'd remembered his sweater. He'd left Anna in bed, sleeping like a baby. She hadn't even woken up when he'd dropped his keys on the floor. Lucky her!

Being out on the sea was beginning to work its magic. As the boat rose and fell gently, Stephen remembered his excitement as a child on fishing trips with his father. His memories of his childhood holidays were of fishing with his father for hours, not saying much but enjoying the activity. It was one of the few times they'd spent a lot of time together. Now it was too late. His father had died a year ago from an unexpected heart attack, leaving Stephen full of things he'd wanted to say to him.

Today, the sea was calm. The sun made the tops of the waves dance and shine. And when Tristan stopped the boat there was silence, no more noise from the engine, just the rather sad sounds from a few seagulls. Together they started fishing off the back of the boat.

After a few minutes Tristan said, 'Got one.'

He pulled in the fish and said, 'Mm, a mackerel. Nothing special, but quite nice grilled on the barbecue. Right, I can relax now. I always think it's a good sign to catch the first fish quickly. I think we're going to have an excellent couple of hours.'

'I hope so,' replied Stephen, 'Anna wants something for tonight's dinner.'

'Are you both OK in Dolphin Cottage? It's not very

modern, I'm afraid. I haven't done much to it, really. My grandmother lived there all her life and she left it to me when she died four years ago.'

'We're absolutely fine. We love it. Actually, I don't think we'll ever want to leave it.'

Tristan looked at him rather sharply.

'Sorry. Have I said something wrong?' said Stephen.

'No, not at all.' Tristan shook his head. 'I was just remembering someone else who said that about the cottage. But in fact she did leave in the end.'

'You're very lucky to live in such a beautiful place. Have you always lived here?' Stephen was interested in getting people to talk about themselves – and it was easier than talking about himself.

'Yes, except when I went away for four years to university.'

Stephen hadn't expected that. Apparently, Tristan had left Polreath when he was eighteen and had been very excited about living in a city. But he'd found that he missed the sea and the open spaces.

'Now, when I have to go to London, I look at people's faces and see how difficult life is for a lot of them,' Tristan explained. 'All that running about and all that fear. You know – fear of crime, fear of losing your job. I couldn't live like that. I've tried and I know. Polreath is home for me. I know it is.'

'Have you got any family here?' asked Stephen.

'Only my sister now,' Tristan replied. My parents moved away when my father retired from fishing. But my sister and I are very close. She's happy here, like me.'

Stephen listened to what Tristan was saying and, for the

first time, he began to feel he understood. Of course, he'd heard other people say how hard city living was, and he'd even said it himself. In fact, last year when they were on their way home from two weeks' holiday in Greece, he'd suggested to Anna that they should sell their house and move to somewhere peaceful. But he'd known it was only a dream. When he'd gone back to the agency the following Monday he found he enjoyed the office politics and the competition for new business – it made him feel alive and at the centre of things. But now, something was different. Perhaps it was because everything at work was so uncertain.

Again, there was silence in the boat. Both men watched the water to see if any fish were biting, and both men were deep in their own thoughts. They each caught some fish – mainly mackerel – and Tristan talked a little more about Polreath and his life there. Stephen liked the easy way in which Tristan talked; he knew that that was how Anna would like *him* to be.

'Well, we'd better go back, I suppose,' said Tristan. 'I've got a trip to do later. How many have you caught?'

'Four. Not bad for a city boy!' Stephen replied.

There was something in Stephen's voice that made Tristan look at him.

Chapter 6   *The phone call*

Anna was in the front garden of Dolphin Cottage and she waved as she saw the boat come in to the harbour.

'You two seem very happy together,' said Tristan.

'Yes,' Stephen agreed. They had known Tristan for only a few days and it seemed to Stephen a rather personal thing to say. But then Stephen realised he didn't mind.

'Have you got anyone special?' he asked.

'Sort of,' Tristan replied, and busied himself tying up the boat to the harbour side. He didn't really feel like going into detail about it at that moment. One reason was that he was thinking about Anna, not Jill.

'Thanks for the trip,' said Stephen. 'It was great. By the way, if you're not doing anything tonight, would you like to come and have dinner with us? We could barbecue the fish. Bring your friend, if you want.'

'OK. Thanks. It'll just be me though,' said Tristan, pleased at the thought of seeing Anna again.

'Fine. See you about eight, then.' Stephen walked up from the harbour, and held up his fish to show Anna. But when he got nearer, he could see that something was wrong.

'What's the matter?' he asked. 'Has something happened?'

'Afraid so. Rebecca's just phoned and said your office need you to ring them immediately.'

'Oh shit! I knew we shouldn't have left our number with

Rebecca!' he said angrily. 'What the hell do they want? I don't feel like ringing them back. I think I just won't, and pretend we never got the message. Do you know if Rebecca told the office she knew where we were?'

'Apparently she said she'd pass the message on to you, so I guess you'll have to contact them.'

'Oh bloody hell.' Stephen threw the fish down on the table and went inside.

She could hear him in the kitchen, noisily making a cup of coffee. She wondered what the problem was at his office. She had met Charlie Jardine, Stephen's boss, a couple of times and he'd seemed to be a reasonable person. What was it all about? Stephen must be talking to him now – she could hear his voice rising in anger, and then she heard him put the phone down with a bang. He came out and sat next to Anna. His face was red with anger.

'Well?' she asked.

'Charlie wants everybody back in the office for a crisis meeting tomorrow. Everybody! And that includes me,' Stephen replied. 'Another agency wants to buy our company.'

'Can't you talk about it on the phone?' Anna asked.

'Apparently, things are happening so quickly and he needs to be able to act fast.' Stephen stood up and started walking up and down the tiny front garden. 'And he says he wants to do what's best for the company. He sounded really worried on the phone.'

'So you're going then,' she said, rather coldly.

'I'll have to. Mark's been called back from a conference in Italy as well.'

'That's work, not a holiday,' said Anna sharply.

'I know. Look, I'm sorry.' Stephen put his arms round her. 'I know this has ruined things for you as well. If I go this morning, I'll come back straight after the meeting. I'll drive through the night if I have to, but I promise I'll be back for breakfast on Thursday.'

'Could you lose your job if someone buys the company?' Anna asked.

'Yes, it's quite possible,' Stephen said. 'It's also possible I could lose it anyway. The agency is obviously in a bad way, as far as money goes.'

'Oh Stephen – just when we were beginning to relax here. It's not fair!' said Anna, close to tears.

Stephen finished his coffee and went back into the cottage. Anna continued to sit in the front garden. Half an hour later, Stephen appeared, carrying a small bag and wearing his work trousers.

'I'll walk with you to the car,' said Anna. It felt unreal to both of them – him going, her staying. She could see that Stephen's mind was already full of work.

The inside of the car was hot from being in the sun, so they opened all the doors to let some air in.

'You'll be OK on your own for two days, won't you?' said Stephen.

'Yes, no problem. Don't worry about me. You just be careful driving. Take care, please.'

'I will. Bye love.'

'Bye. I don't know what to say . . . good luck, I suppose. Ring me tonight from home – I want to know you're there.'

Anna watched Stephen drive away. 'Poor man,' she thought, and then selfishly, 'I'm pleased I don't have to go, too.'

Chapter 7   *Tristan comes for dinner*

Anna had a pleasant day. It was difficult not to. Polreath was the same interesting place and the weather was wonderful again. She walked around and did a bit of shopping. Some people in the village were beginning to greet her, 'Morning. Another nice day,' they said, and she smiled back.

She sat in the front garden of the cottage, reading and watching all the comings and goings in the harbour. She was learning to recognise some of the different boats – which ones were fishing boats, and which ones were owned by visitors. Tristan's boat, full of passengers, went out, and she decided she'd find out where he was going the next day. It might be nice to do something with other people tomorrow, she thought.

She looked at Stephen's fish in the fridge and remembered how pleased he'd looked when he'd got off Tristan's boat earlier that day. 'I'll have some later,' she thought. 'Don't want to waste them.'

In the late afternoon, she went for a swim. Back home, she showered and sat with a glass of white wine in the front garden until the sun disappeared behind the hill. Then she went inside to get some dinner.

There was a knock on the door, and Tristan appeared. 'Hello, I hope I'm not late.'

'Pardon?' said Anna. 'Late for what?'

'Dinner. Stephen asked me for dinner.' Tristan could see something was wrong. 'Oh, no! I can see you didn't know!'

'I'm sorry. Come in. No, I didn't know. The thing is,' explained Anna, 'Stephen's had to go back to London. He had a phone call when you were out fishing this morning, and he's gone.'

'Oh, I'm sorry. Is everything all right . . .? I mean, I hope nothing bad has happened.' Tristan meant what he said, but if he was honest with himself, he was also pleased that Anna was now here alone, without Stephen.

'It's a crisis at work,' Anna said. 'He didn't want to leave but . . . He'll be back on Thursday, he says.'

'Oh good. Anyway, I'll go. Don't worry about dinner,' said Tristan.

'No, stay, really,' she said. 'I was just grilling the fish. I can easily do some more. Help yourself to a glass of wine.'

'Well, if you're sure. Thanks.' Tristan poured himself a drink and filled up Anna's glass as well.

'Can I do anything?' he asked.

'You could cut the bread, if you want. And take all the plates and stuff outside. Is it OK with you if we eat outside?'

'Fine.' Tristan carried everything into the front garden and waited for Anna. He felt a bit strange sitting there, remembering other times he'd had dinner at the cottage. Jill and he used to eat there most evenings during their first summer together. But when she was here earlier this year, though, she seemed to prefer to eat at *his* house or in the village somewhere. The cottage had become Jill's private world. Anna brought the fish. Strange, he thought, to himself. There's Jill and Stephen in London and Anna and me here. Tristan talked a bit about his day. After the fishing that morning, he'd been quite busy – two trips with a full boat each time, up the coast looking at the land from the sea. He seemed surprised when she asked him if he ever got bored doing the same trips every week. 'Never bored,' he said. 'Annoyed maybe at some of the stupid questions people ask sometimes. But basically I can't think of a better way of earning a living.'

The phone rang and made them both jump. 'That'll be Stephen, I hope,' said Anna and went to answer it. Tristan sat and thought how much he liked Anna's company.

She came back out a few minutes later. 'Yes, it was. He said sorry about tonight – about forgetting to tell me you were coming to dinner. And he says London is hot, airless and dirty!'

'Does he enjoy his job, whatever it is?' asked Tristan.

'He works for an advertising agency. To be honest, I don't know if he does enjoy it any more. He used to, but recently something's changed. Maybe he's changed. He was hoping – well, actually, I was hoping – this holiday would give him a chance to have a good think about it all. Perhaps now, the decisions will be taken for him. He may come back on Thursday without a job. But, I'm sorry, you probably don't want to hear all that. You were just being polite.'

'No, I wasn't . . . if you understand me. I'm interested. I like the little I know about Stephen. I enjoyed our fishing trip this morning.' Tristan paused and then said, 'Maybe it's my turn to be honest. You see, you and Stephen make me think about myself and my . . . I don't know what to call her – woman-friend, girl-friend, whatever.' Anna waited for him to go on. He told her about Jill and him and the difficulties of continuing a long-distance relationship. He spoke quite openly about it all. Anna couldn't help comparing him with Stephen. Stephen always had such difficulty trying to explain something personal. The death of his father had hit him hard but he still hadn't really talked about it with her. Only once, about three months ago, when she'd found him in the kitchen crying, then he'd managed to talk about it a bit. Poor darling Stephen, people who only saw his public face just didn't know him.

They opened another bottle of wine and carried on talking – about him, about her and Stephen, about the village and the people who lived there.

Finally Tristan stood up. 'It's time I went. Thank you for a really nice evening. You're a good listener.'

'So are you.'

'Shall I see you tomorrow?' he asked.

'Yes, I was thinking of coming on one of your trips. Where are you going in the morning?' asked Anna.

'Out past Skellig and round the rocks.' He took a step nearer her. 'It's a good trip. The boat leaves at ten.'

'Fine. I'll be there.' Maybe it was the wine, but he seemed to be standing closer. He put his hands on her shoulders and kissed her quite firmly on the lips.

'Goodnight. See you in the morning,' he said, and closed the gate behind him.

Chapter 8   *On Wave Dancer*

When Anna woke the next morning, she forgot that Stephen wasn't in bed next to her until she turned over to touch him. She looked at her watch – eight o'clock. He'd be on his way to the office now, probably caught in traffic. Poor thing. She lay there for a while thinking about him and wondering how much today would change their lives.

'Coffee,' she thought. 'And I think I'll go and get the newspaper. I can do the crossword before I go on the trip.'

On her way down to the shop, she started thinking about last night's dinner with Tristan. She wondered if today they'd be as easy with each other as they'd been last night. The woman in the shop said, 'Morning. Did you have a nice dinner last night?'

'Yes, thank you,' said Anna in a surprised voice.

The woman continued, 'I saw you when I was walking my dog. You can't keep anything secret in this place for long!'

Anna laughed. 'I must remember that,' she thought.

Back home, she tried the crossword but it was too difficult, so she left it for later. She could see Tristan's boat below with Tristan on board. She noticed there was more movement on the sea today. It wasn't rough but the boats were moving up and down a little.

She went inside to collect her backpack from the cottage

and went down to the harbour. Tristan was by the boat, talking to another man.

'Morning, Anna,' said Tristan. 'Everything OK? This is Gary – he works with me on the boat trips. Anna's staying at Dolphin Cottage,' he said to Gary.

They smiled at each other. Gary looked at her quite closely and she wondered if they'd been talking about her when she arrived.

'I haven't got a ticket or anything for this trip,' said Anna. 'Do I need one?'

'No,' replied Gary. 'You pay on the boat. Have you got a jacket or something with you? You might need it today. We were just saying that the sea'll probably be a bit rough on the other side of the island.'

'The water comes over the boat in certain places. Sit near the front on the right side if you don't want to get wet,' Tristan added.

'Right. Thanks.'

He jumped onto the boat and then turned to help Anna. He held out his hand and took hers very firmly. He kept hold until she had sat down. Other people were now arriving and getting on the boat. Most of them seemed to know Tristan. Perhaps they went on his trips often. Anna recognised one or two who she'd seen on the beach or in the village somewhere. Everybody seemed very well-prepared – jackets, extra sweaters, binoculars, cameras. Ready for a trans-Atlantic expedition, she thought. Then she looked at Tristan and Gary in their shorts and T-shirts and wondered which group had got it right.

Tristan started explaining to everyone where they were going and what they might see on the trip. This gave her a good chance to look at him carefully. He told a few funny stories and the passengers laughed in the right places. Anna found herself thinking how attractive he was – and not just physically. He had an air of confidence about him that she liked. But then, he must have felt Anna's eyes on him because he turned towards her and she blushed! She could feel her cheeks going red! Just like a schoolgirl caught doing something wrong! How embarrassing!

As soon as they left the harbour, the sea became much rougher but nobody seemed to be worried. In fact, it was quite fun trying to move your body with the movement of the boat – a bit like riding a horse, Anna thought. Once or twice, when the boat went into a wave, water came over the side, and again, people seemed to think it was all part of the fun. They passed the island and moved on towards the rocks. From Polreath, you couldn't really see very much beyond the island so Anna was surprised at the size of some of the rocks – almost like mini-islands. Tristan took the boat close in and slowed the engine.

'There are very often seals around here. In fact, we might see some young ones – the first ones are usually born around this time,' he said quietly.

'Look!' said a man at the back of the boat. 'There are two in the water over there.'

Everybody focused their binoculars where he was pointing. The heads of two adult seals appeared and then disappeared behind a wave. Someone tried to take a picture.

Tristan took the boat in and out of the rocks. They managed to see some seals out of the water – lying on rocks, almost sunbathing – but no young ones. They were about to turn for home when Gary saw something white on the rocks just above the water. It was a very young seal.

'Don't make too much noise,' said Tristan. 'We don't want to frighten it, or worry its Mum, wherever she is. This is the first one I've seen this year. I guess it's only a few days old.'

Not many people on the boat had ever seen a young seal before so they were really pleased. Anna thought how helpless it looked, all by itself on the rock. And as if he knew what she was thinking, Tristan said, 'The first few days are dangerous ones for the young. Some of the bigger seabirds attack them – they go for their eyes.'

The boat was moving up and down quite a lot and it was difficult to stand. Suddenly, the boat was caught by a bigger wave and an elderly woman fell sideways. In trying to save herself, she hit her arm on the side. Immediately, people crowded round her, and started talking:

'Are you all right?'

'Here, let's get you up onto a seat.'

'Just sit quietly for a minute. What a nasty shock!'

Tristan moved the boat out into deeper water, away from the rocks. He looked at Anna and his eyes seemed to be asking her 'Could you?' She went over to the woman.

'Would you like me to look?' she said. 'I'm a nurse.'

'I'm all right,' she said. 'I think I just hurt my arm, that's all.'

Anna moved the woman and her husband up to the front of the boat. She looked at the arm which was quite red and already beginning to get bigger. Very gently, she pressed and the woman made a small sound.

'Well, Mrs ... er ...' Anna began.

'Taylor . . . Sheila,' the woman said.

'Sheila, I don't think you've broken it, but it'd be a good idea to have it X-rayed when we get back, just to make sure.' Anna looked up. 'Tristan, where's the nearest place for that?'

'The Cottage Hospital in Kingham – it's not far. I'll take you in the car, Mrs Taylor.'

Anna found a bandage in the First Aid box and tied Mrs Taylor's arm up. The poor old woman had gone a bit white now and was shaking. Someone passed her a cup of tea. I was right, thought Anna, they came prepared for anything! By the time they reached Polreath, Mrs Taylor looked better but her arm was clearly giving her a lot of pain. Fortunately, Tristan's car was near the harbour and Mr and Mrs Taylor got in the back.

'Would you like me to come too?' asked Anna.

'Please,' said Tristan. He looked more worried than anybody. I wonder if he's insured for accidents, she thought. I suppose something like this is not good for his business.

The X-ray showed bruising but the arm wasn't broken.

'I'm really sorry, Mrs Taylor,' said Tristan.

'It's not your fault,' she replied. 'You're not responsible for the sea. I shouldn't have been standing up.'

'Well, let's go back home. I'll buy everyone a drink when we get back. I think we all need one,' Tristan said.

The Taylors didn't want a drink, so Tristan and Anna left them at their hotel.

'Your arm will hurt a lot tonight,' said Anna. 'So take some aspirins before you go to bed – they'll help with the pain.'

'Thank you for your help,' said Mr Taylor. 'We'll probably see you around somewhere in the next day or two.'

'Poor old thing,' said Anna, drinking her beer in the Fisherman's Arms. 'She was lucky today. But I don't think she'll be doing much for the next couple of days. That arm'll hurt for a bit.'

'I was lucky,' replied Tristan, with a shake of the head. 'It's fortunate she was so nice about it – someone different might have complained and spread the word about. People would soon begin to think I was a bit careless with my passengers, and there are one or two people in this village who would be quite happy to see me lose business.'

'Really? Why?' asked Anna.

'Oh, jealousy, I suppose,' Tristan replied. 'It's a small place, Polreath; feelings get a bit strong sometimes.'

'Have they got reason to be jealous?' Anna asked, remembering the conversation that she and Stephen had heard in the bar the other day.

'Well,' he laughed, 'I'm not sure I'm the best person to answer that! You should ask them! People might think I've got a good life – what with the boat and two cottages.'

'And maybe a third cottage to come?' Anna added.

'Why do you say that?' Tristan asked sharply.

'Sorry, I shouldn't have. I was just repeating something we heard about you in here the other day,' Anna said, wishing she hadn't asked. 'A guy called Jack was saying that you were interested in another cottage in the village.'

'Ah ha, Jack! There you are, you see. The stories that spread in a small village!' Tristan looked a bit angry.

'Look, I'm sorry,' Anna said quickly. 'It's none of my business. Shall we change the subject? I meant to say earlier how much I enjoyed the trip – except for the accident, of course. You made it interesting for everyone.'

'Thanks.' There was a bit of an uncomfortable silence. Tristan stared into his beer and then said, 'I don't want another cottage. I was interested in the price because it's more or less the same size as Dolphin Cottage. And I wanted to know how much I might be able to sell that for.'

'You want to sell Dolphin Cottage?' said Anna in complete surprise. 'Oh don't! It's too lovely to lose.'

'I don't really know whether I want to or not – I might need to, to get some money. It's got some rather mixed memories for me – Jill, you know. And as you now understand, owning two places can cause bad feeling.

'Anyway, I've got to go. Believe it or not, I've got another trip to do – a quick one-hour up the coast.' He waited a second or two before continuing. 'But I was wondering, if you're not doing anything tonight, can I buy you dinner – to thank you for dinner last night, and for Mrs Taylor?'

He looked at her carefully to see what she would say. Would she think he was just being friendly or more than that? He meant it to be friendly, but he had an awful feeling he wanted more.

'Thank you. I'd like that,' she said returning his look.

'I thought we could drive to a place in the next village – it'd be a change. Meet in the car park at eight?'

'Fine. Have a safe trip this afternoon!' She ordered a coffee and sat there, wondering what she was doing, and feeling guilty because she hadn't really thought about Stephen all day.

Chapter 9   *Dinner at Gino's*

'Someone's going to buy the company,' said Stephen on the phone from London. And then he said something about it being 'the best thing all round'. He sounded quite cheerful, said he would be with her in the morning and that he missed her. Anna felt, in all honesty, that she couldn't say the same thing back to him. Today had been so full of other things that she hadn't really missed him.

So all she said to him was, 'It'll be lovely to see you for breakfast' – which was true, it would be lovely – Stephen was the most important person in her life. But she didn't say anything about going out with Tristan.

She put on a bright red dress that she'd had for years but which always made her feel great, especially when she had a suntan, and gave her hair a quick brush. She was excited about tonight. It was a great feeling getting ready to go out with another man. It reminded her of how she felt before she met Stephen.

She walked slowly up the hill to the car park.

'Hey, you look nice,' said Anna when she saw Tristan. Instead of his usual shorts and T-shirt Tristan was wearing trousers and a green short-sleeved shirt. 'We're not going anywhere expensive, are we?' she asked.

'No, just an Italian restaurant in St Leven, not far. And you look wonderful!' Tristan replied. 'Shall we go?'

Tristan's car smelt of fish. The whole of the back was full

of nets. 'Does it smell?' he asked when he saw Anna's face. 'It just seems normal to me.'

'Well, I'm just glad we're not going far,' laughed Anna.

'Sorry. Actually, all I can smell is your perfume. Have you heard from Stephen?' asked Tristan.

'Yes, he just rang,' replied Anna. 'He seemed fine. He said he'd be back tomorrow for breakfast.'

'Is he driving down overnight, then?' asked Tristan.

'Yes, I guess so. He likes night driving.'

It took about fifteen minutes to get to St Leven. Anna suggested going for a walk round the harbour first. She needed a bit of fresh air after the fishy car. The harbour was bigger than Polreath and so were the fishing boats. One or two of the men on board said hello to Tristan and gave Anna a quick look. 'I get the feeling I'm being noticed,' Anna thought. 'I wonder if that woman in the shop in Polreath is going to tell me tomorrow what I was doing tonight!'

'What are you smiling at?' asked Tristan.

'I was just thinking how hard it would be to keep anything secret down here,' Anna replied.

'True. Were you thinking about anything in particular?' he asked, looking at her.

'No,' she lied. 'Let's go and eat. I'm really hungry.'

Gino's restaurant was away from the sea, in a narrow street. They walked through the restaurant to the garden at the back where there were a number of tables gathered around a pizza oven. Gino was putting in and taking out the pizzas from the oven with a long wooden thing.

' 'ello, Tristan. Good to see you. 'ow are you?' said Gino.

Tristan and Anna sat at the only free table and ordered

two pizza margheritas and the house wine. They began talking about Italy, where they had both been, and then the difficulty of living away from your own country. Tristan said it was not 'the country' that was important for him but simply the place where you were – the town, the village.

'And that's why Jill and I can never work as a couple. Neither of us is willing to leave the place where we want to be. We spoke on the phone earlier today and decided to be realistic. We haven't really got a future together. I'm sure we'll try to remain friends. There was a lot between us and we had good laughs. But everybody says that kind of thing when their relationship breaks up.'

'I'm sorry it didn't work out for you,' said Anna.

'Actually, you helped me to take the decision,' said Tristan, and looked across at Anna to see what she would do. She was looking directly at him so he continued. 'This is going to sound like a Hollywood movie but ... you've woken me up.' Tristan reached across the table and took her hand. 'I was feeling really sorry for myself and then you and Stephen arrived.'

'Yes, me *and Stephen*,' Anna repeated. And yes, it did sound like a film, she thought, but she wanted him to continue. 'What's so special about me and Stephen? You must meet hundreds of visitors every year, and they probably all fall in love with Polreath, and half of them with you too.'

'I don't know why. I just know I wanted to get to know you both better. Maybe you arrived at the right time, I don't know. Anyway, whatever it is, I feel clearer about some things.'

'I don't,' thought Anna. 'I feel confused. Why is he holding my hand? Would he be holding Stephen's hand too if he was here?'

'But now there's another problem,' he went on. 'I think we're attracted to one another.'

Anna pulled her hand away. How could he say that! He'd just been talking about her and Stephen and now he was saying this. How could he? Five minutes ago he'd been talking about breaking up with Jill. That can't have been easy to do. And here he was, saying he was attracted to her. It sounded like throwing off one pair of shoes and trying on a new pair. What was he doing?

'I'm sorry. I shouldn't have said that.'

'No, you shouldn't,' said Anna.

'But it's true, isn't it?' Tristan said softly.

'Yes.' And she picked up her glass to hide her confusion. 'But I don't intend to do anything about it. I'm with Stephen and we're happy. And you've confused me.'

'Same here,' he said. He took hold of her hand again. 'I know you're happy with Stephen – I could see it the first day you were here. I just thought it was better to bring everything out into the open. Sometimes if you don't talk about things they become even more important.'

'Maybe some things are better left unsaid. Stephen's coming back tomorrow and in three weeks I'll have disappeared out of your life. Oh, I don't know what I'm doing anymore,' Anna said.

'It's not a crime to find someone attractive, is it?' he said.

'No, it's not. In fact, it's great in a way. But I've been with Stephen for ten years and this is the first time I've been in this situation. I don't know what to do. And by the way, Gino is looking at us. Let's talk about something else, please.'

And they did. They talked about food and they slowly relaxed. But all the time Anna was thinking. She *did* find him attractive and if there were no Stephen, who knows what might happen. Recently she had felt excluded sometimes by Stephen. He had seemed to be in a world of his own, so it was wonderful to be the centre of Tristan's attention.

Tristan's thoughts were going along similar lines. He didn't want to hurt anybody. Maybe he should have kept his mouth shut. That was his problem – he always had to say what he was thinking, didn't he? It had got him into trouble more than once in the past. Anna was a warm, open, lively woman – and he felt good when he was with her. But, as she said, she would be leaving in three weeks, so there was no point in letting things go any further.

They got up to leave and Gino came over. 'Cheerio, my friend,' he said, 'and my friend's friend,' he said looking at Anna. ' 'ope to see you again. Be good!'

'Mmm, an interesting choice of words,' thought Tristan as they stepped out into the street.

'Gosh, Tristan, the smell of fish in your car is quite powerful. We'll have to drive with the windows open,' said Anna. Sitting in the car on the way back to Polreath was not very easy. And it wasn't just because of the fishy smell. They were both very conscious of each other sitting close by. Tristan parked the car above the village and they got out.

'Let's just walk for a bit,' said Anna. 'I don't want to go back to the cottage yet.'

They took the path along the top of the cliffs. It was dark but the moon was bright enough so there was no danger of them walking over the edge. In places the path was quite narrow where it passed between bushes and Anna walked in front. Being in front made her feel as if she was in charge of the situation. Then she heard something move just ahead, an animal probably, and she stopped suddenly. Tristan walked into the back of her. She jumped and half turned round. They were standing so close. She reached up and touched his face with her finger. He put his arms round her and they kissed, long and hard.

Anna pulled away from him. 'So much for not letting things go any further,' said Tristan softly.

'I think I knew that was going to happen,' said Anna. The sense of his body was still with her. 'I know this might sound odd, but I needed that!'

Tristan smiled. 'So did I – and I need more.' They kissed again but this time more lightly. It was almost as if a spell had been broken, and a deep and exciting kiss had been enough for the moment.

'Anna, I think you're wonderful,' he said, trying to keep his voice light. 'I wish we were free to do whatever we want, but we're not. At least, I'll still be able to look Stephen in the eye when I see him tomorrow.'

'I hope I can, too. Do you think we'd better go before anything else happens? We don't need to say anything to Stephen, either of us, do we?'

'No, why should we?' he replied. 'Nothing's happened.'

But they both knew something had.

Chapter 10 *Stephen's return*

Anna woke up because she felt something on her cheek. She pushed it away.

'Ouch! That's my nose!' Stephen cried.

She opened her eyes and there was Stephen bending over her and rubbing his nose where she'd hit it.

'Hello, love,' said Anna. 'You're back. What time is it?'

'Seven. Sorry to wake you but you looked so lovely lying there. I'll go and make some coffee and bring it up. It's a beautiful morning.'

Anna lay there, listening to Stephen downstairs, and remembering the night before. She felt good. She'd had an 'adventure' and she had escaped. Now Stephen was back and everything would be back to normal.

He sat on the bed drinking coffee and told her about the agency meeting. Everyone had all agreed in the end that the sale of the company was the best thing. The buyers had been honest about the future and said there were no guarantees of people keeping their jobs. There would have to be some restructuring – which, according to Stephen, meant a lot of people losing their jobs.

'So, we're going to have a few months without knowing whether I'll be one of the lucky ones,' said Stephen.

'Well, you look very cheerful about it,' replied Anna.

'There's nothing I can do. It's out of my hands. So to hell with it all, for the moment. I don't even know if I want to keep the job anyway,' Stephen said as he started to get undressed. 'I'm going to have a shower, and then maybe have a few hours' sleep.'

Anna was surprised. Stephen didn't really seem worried about it all. 'How amazing! Perhaps he *is* changing,' she thought. She decided to get up. She didn't feel like lying in bed waiting for Stephen. It was better to be active. She made another cup of coffee and stood outside listening to the morning sounds. Tristan was on his boat, doing something with a fishing net. 'Probably one of the smelly ones from the car,' she thought.

How did she feel about him this morning? Quite relaxed, she thought, although something was making her heart beat faster. 'Must be the coffee,' she said to herself, and went inside to get some breakfast.

'Did you have a good evening with Tristan?' Stephen was sitting at the kitchen table. He stood up and put his arms round Anna.

'Mm, yes, I did,' said Anna, wondering for a moment which evening he was talking about. 'Yes, it was fun. He's very good to be with – and very open about everything, isn't he? It doesn't seem to worry him that he's only just met us. Anyway, what are you doing – I thought you were going to have a bit of sleep?'

'Changed my mind,' replied Stephen. 'The bed seemed empty, and I don't want to waste the day sleeping. I want to start my holiday again. Do you feel like going surfing later? If we walk over there, you can tell me what you've been doing while I've been away.'

Anna had already decided that she was going to tell him about last night's dinner. She knew if she didn't, he was sure to hear about it from someone else – half the population of Polreath and St Leven probably. So, as they walked over to the surf beach, she told him all about going on the boat out to the rocks, and the accident and about Gino's, and even about Tristan and Jill splitting up. But she missed out the walk at the end of the evening. She could feel Stephen looking at her once or twice.

'Well, you have been busy,' he said thoughtfully. She seemed to have been perfectly happy without him. 'You obviously enjoyed it all. You like Tristan, don't you?'

'Yes – don't you?' she replied.

'Yes, at least, what I know of him,' said Stephen slowly. 'I like the way he lives and the way he seems to know what makes him happy. That's quite rare.' Anna waited; she realised that Stephen hadn't finished. 'Did he tell you he went to university – he got a degree in civil engineering? He was offered a good job, too, but he didn't take it. He wanted to come back to Polreath instead. He could have been really successful by now – probably a manager with a high salary. But he knew that wasn't really for him,' Stephen paused. Now it was Anna's turn to look at him.

'What are you saying?' asked Anna.

'Nothing really – just that I think he made the right decision – for him,' Stephen said.

'Are you trying to tell me you feel you've made the wrong decision? I always thought you loved the advertising world – and life in the city,' said Anna.

'I do . . . I did.' Stephen stopped for a moment. 'All I'm saying is I think I've reached a crossroads in my life. I feel it's time for a change of direction. Maybe it's a mid-life crisis – I don't know.'

'You're too young for a mid-life crisis,' replied Anna. 'Have you got any ideas about what you'd like to do, then?'

'One or two but they're still just ideas, so I don't really want to talk about them yet.'

'I've heard that before,' thought Anna.

Stephen continued, 'I need time to think more. Everything's happened so quickly.'

'Not *that* quickly, actually,' she said. 'You've seemed different the last few weeks. I think this has been coming for a while.'

'You're probably right. But don't push me to say more at the moment, will you? I need time.'

They walked on in silence, busy with their own thoughts. Anna wasn't surprised by what Stephen had said. She just hoped he'd talk to her more before taking any big decisions. After all, it affected her life, too.

The surf beach was busy when they got there.

'I'm ready for this,' said Stephen, 'after the last forty-eight hours, I need action.'

They went to the beach shop and hired surfboards. Neither of them felt like having a lesson – they wanted to try it themselves first. They swam out with the boards to just beyond the point where the waves were starting. Then they watched to see what other people did. Timing was the important thing. You had to catch the right wave at exactly the right time. If you missed it, there was nothing to carry you in towards the beach. You had to try again, wait for the next suitable wave. It was fun. They couldn't really do it well, but they enjoyed trying. Stephen did manage to stand up on his board for about ten seconds but Anna was perfectly happy lying down on the board, surfing in on her stomach.

'I've had enough,' shouted Anna. 'I'm giving up for the moment.' She lay on the sand and let the sun warm her. Then she sat up to watch Stephen. He was doing quite well. But then he often did do well at sport. She could see he wanted to be good at this.

'I enjoyed that,' said Stephen, lying down on the beach beside her. 'When you get it right, it's a great feeling!' Turning over, he put his cold, wet hands on Anna's stomach.

'Ohhhh! You horror! Your hands are freezing!'

He laughed, and pulled her to her feet. 'Time for lunch. I could eat a horse.'

They carried their surfboards to the open-air café and 'parked' them next to some others. They had burgers and French fries with lots of ketchup, and enjoyed every mouthful of it. 'God, that was wonderful – just what I needed,' said Stephen. 'OK. What do you want to do now, then? I'd quite like to go back to the cottage. My sleepless night is catching up with me. I'm beginning to feel really tired.'

'That's fine with me. I'm very happy sitting in the front garden watching the world. I've got yesterday's crossword to finish, too.'

Chapter 11   *Back to normal*

Stephen went upstairs for a rest when they got home. He asked Anna to wake him in a couple of hours. She took her coffee, newspaper, book and suntan cream into the garden and made herself comfortable. The sun felt good on her skin. She felt totally happy and couldn't imagine ever wanting anything more. 'It'd probably be better,' she thought, 'if we didn't see Tristan today. Just give me time to get myself in balance again. It seems as if that man is having an interesting effect on both Stephen and me. I think Stephen knows I'm attracted to him, and Stephen obviously likes him too.'

At about five o'clock, she took a cup of tea to Stephen to wake him up. He was fast asleep.

'Teatime,' she whispered in his ear. He opened one eye and stared at her standing there in her swimsuit.

'How nice to be woken up by a half-naked woman with a cup of tea. Why don't you join me in here, it's lovely.' She got in and they made love. They knew each other so well – it was all so familiar, not passionate but comfortable and loving.

'I'd like to stay here for ever,' said Stephen.

'What, in bed?'

'No, in Polreath,' he laughed. 'It suits us both – you look wonderful and I feel better than I have for months.'

'You said the same last year when we were in Greece – remember?'

'Did I?' said Stephen, getting out of bed. 'Oh well, this is different, I think.'

It was late afternoon and they went down to the beach for a lazy swim. They called at the shop and sure enough the woman said, 'What did you think of Gino's then, Mrs Martins?'

'I knew it,' thought Anna, 'I knew she would say something. It's a good thing I told Stephen or I'd be in trouble now.' She answered the woman in her sweetest voice.

Outside the shop, Stephen suggested going for a drink.

'No, let's go back home.' Anna was surprised to find she felt bad about the woman's comments. In any case, she didn't think she wanted to meet Tristan at the moment.

They spent a pleasant evening at home. Stephen cooked an amazing fish pie, and they ate outside even though the evening was not quite as warm as before. 'I'd like a quick beer in the pub before bedtime. Do you want to come?' asked Stephen.

'No, I'll stay here. You won't be long, will you?'

Ten minutes after Stephen left, the phone rang. 'If that's anybody from London from Stephen's office, I'll probably shout at them,' thought Anna as she stood up. 'Why don't they leave him alone?'

'Hello!' she said very roughly.

'Hello. God, you sound angry!' It was Tristan.

'Oh hello, Tristan. Sorry, I thought it was going to be someone else. Sorry. What ..., I mean, why ...?' and she didn't know how to finish.

'You mean why am I ringing?' Tristan finished her question for her. 'Well, I saw Stephen going into the

Fisherman's Arms so I thought I'd just check to see if you ... if everything's OK.'

'Yes, I think so,' she said. 'Stephen's happy to be back. In fact, I thought when the phone rang it was going to be someone about his work – that's why I sounded angry. Is everything OK with you?'

'Yes, fine.' A pause. 'The other reason I rang was to remind you that there's another trip to Skellig tomorrow morning if you're interested. It'd be nice to see you, both of you, I think.' Tristan sounded a bit embarrassed.

'Right. We'll probably come – I'll mention it to Stephen when he gets back. What's the weather forecast for tomorrow?' asked Anna. 'I thought it was a bit cooler tonight. It's not going to change, is it?'

'No, not yet,' he replied. 'We've got the good weather for a bit longer, so they say.'

'Look, Tristan. Why don't you go and join Stephen in the bar? He'd like to see you, I know, and it might be a good idea to see him without me around for the first time since we ... you know ...' and again, Anna couldn't finish.

'Mm, that's probably a good idea,' said Tristan brightly. 'Thanks. I won't say anything about ringing you tonight. And I'll mention the trip to Skellig to him. OK? Goodnight, Anna. See you tomorrow, I hope.'

Anna was pleased with herself for being so strongminded, but she was shaking a bit when she put the phone down. Then she thought it was quite funny, really. Last night with her – tonight with Stephen. Tristan was certainly being very equal in sharing himself between them. She hoped the woman from the shop would see them together!

Chapter 12 *Decision time*

The next day they went on Tristan's trip to Skellig. About fifty people lived on the island all year, and there was one hotel and a few holiday cottages. It took them about an hour to walk around the island which, as Tristan had said, did seem to have something special about it. It was difficult to say exactly what it was. Maybe all small islands had it. The far side, away from the coast, was the best. There was nothing to be seen except the rocks where Anna had been a few days ago. Just ocean, going on for ever.

After their walk, they sat on the beach and discussed whether they could live there. This was a game they often played when they went somewhere new. Stephen thought he could, if he had some work to do, but Anna didn't think she'd like it. 'I'd be worried, I might not like any of the other forty-eight people living here. It's not many to choose from,' she said.

About half an hour before the boat was leaving, they saw Tristan walking over the beach towards them.

'It's a beautiful place, isn't it?' said Tristan, sitting down with them.

'Yes,' replied Stephen.

'Stephen thinks he could live here,' said Anna, 'but I'm quite sure I couldn't.'

'Well that's good, because the islanders wouldn't be too

happy about outsiders moving in. It'd take about twenty years before you were accepted.'

Tristan sat there for a few minutes. Being in Anna's company again that day had affected him. He remembered last night – the taste of her lips, the smell of her perfume. He turned to look at them both and said,

'Now, if you really want to live down here how about buying Dolphin Cottage?'

'Are you serious?' asked Stephen. 'Why do you want to sell?'

'I'm going to have to buy a new boat for next year,' said Tristan. 'This one's OK at the moment, but if I'm serious about making more of a business out of the trips, I really need a better boat – and they cost a lot. Selling the cottage would give me the money I need. But I'm not in any hurry to sell – I just thought I'd throw it into the conversation – give you something to think about!' Tristan's face showed nothing of what he really felt.

'Wouldn't it be the same – you know, not being accepted by the locals in Polreath?' Anna asked.

'It would be less of a problem than on Skellig, because there are already one or two outsiders living in the village,' explained Tristan. 'And of course Dolphin Cottage has been a holiday place for a few years. But it's true, we do have to watch it – you know, make sure the villagers are not pushed out.'

'Hey, wait a minute,' said Stephen with a smile. 'This conversation is going too fast. We live in London, Anna – remember? Your job's there, our friends are there. I don't know about my job, but it's there at the moment. I know I said I was ready for a change but I'm not sure if this is the one I was thinking of.' Stephen's look to Anna said 'I'm interested but we need to talk about it together – later.'

On the journey back, nobody said anything more about the cottage. Anna realised that the possibility of living in Polreath excited her. She started thinking about what work opportunities there were for nurses down here. She also wondered if Tristan really wanted to sell to *anyone* or just to them as a way of keeping in touch with her. Maybe it was asking for trouble even to think about it.

* * *

A wonderful holiday or a new way of life? That was on their minds for the next few days. For Stephen and Anna there were days when they seemed to do nothing except eat, sleep, read and lie in the sun. There were other days when they were more active: Stephen did some more surfing and became quite good. Anna quietly, without telling anyone, found out about jobs for nurses in the area – just in case. The two of them talked about the possibility of buying the cottage. But if they did, would they keep it as a holiday home or move there to live? Stephen told Anna that after the sale of the company, one of his hopes was that the new owners would *not* want to keep him. They couldn't make him leave, so they'd have to offer him some money and he could then use that money to start again. The idea of doing something in the Polreath area attracted him.

'Can we afford to buy this place?' asked Anna.

'Yes,' replied Stephen, 'if we sell the flat in London.'

'But what about work down here?' asked Anna. 'You'd have to do something, we can't live off one salary.'

'I know. That's what I've been thinking about. I want to see if I could work in advertising down here. I'd even be interested in possibly starting a small agency of my own. Or perhaps I could do something with Tristan – possibly get a new boat together or something. What do you think?' Stephen felt quite good about this idea.

'Find out about the advertising world in this area first, because that's what you know about,' said Anna. 'But if you meant what do I think about me and my life, well to be honest I've already got some information about nursing around here. There's a hospital about fifty kilometres away and there's a health centre nearer, in Kingham, so I could work from here.'

'Ah ha! You're a quiet one!' Stephen said. 'You never told me you were doing that! But seriously, what do you think about leaving London, and everyone there?'

'A bit nervous, but definitely interested,' replied Anna. 'I think I'm ready for a change, too.' She remembered she had thought this on her last day at work. 'And this place has become special, hasn't it?'

They went on talking like this for the next few days. Tristan didn't ask them anything about their plans, but they did ask him if he was serious about selling Dolphin Cottage.

'Yes,' he replied, 'but only to the right people. Either a local person or, as I've said before, you two.'

In the middle of the last week of their holiday they felt they'd reached some sort of decision. They'd ask Tristan if they could buy the cottage. Other decisions were going to take longer to make, and even longer to organise, but this was a start.

They met Tristan that evening in the Fisherman's Arms and told him they wanted to go ahead.

'Great,' said Tristan. He and Stephen shook hands, and Tristan kissed Anna on the cheek. He smelt a little bit of fish, which immediately reminded her of his car and their evening together.

'Are you going to live in it all the time?' he asked.

'Eventually, yes,' said Anna quickly. Stephen looked at her in surprise. 'But we've got a lot of things to do first, like sell the flat in London and sort out our jobs ... and things.'

The three of them said goodbye, promising to discuss the details the next day.

'Why did you tell him we were going to live in it all the time? I thought we hadn't really decided that,' said Stephen.

'I had the feeling it was the right thing to say. He doesn't really want it to be just a holiday place. I think he feels better about not selling it to a villager if he knows it's going to become someone's home.' They walked slowly up to the door of Dolphin Cottage. 'In any case, I think we *had* decided in our own minds,' she added.

Chapter 13   *A visit from Jill*

'I see she's back then.' This was the welcome that Anna got when she went into the shop the next morning.

'Here we go again,' she thought, 'more gossip. Still I'd better try to be polite if we're going to live here.' The woman would be a bad enemy to have.

'Who's that, Mrs Lennox. Who's back?' Anna asked.

'Tristan's friend – Jill. I saw her coming down the hill early this morning. Went to his house, she did.' Mrs Lennox looked carefully at Anna to see what she thought of this news. Anna tried to show nothing on her face.

'That's nice. I'm sure he'll be pleased to see her,' she managed to say.

She then had a quick conversation with Mrs Lennox about whether to buy brown bread or white, and what the weather was going to be like for the weekend.

Outside, she decided not to take the direct way back to the cottage, but to go round the harbour. She needed to calm down. The news of Jill's arrival had shaken her. She'd felt over the past week or so that she could control her feelings for Tristan. OK, she liked him, but her feelings for Stephen were stronger and deeper and she'd really felt there wouldn't be any difficulty between the three of them. Now she felt mixed up again. All sorts of things were going through her head. Had Tristan known Jill was coming and hadn't said anything? How long was she staying? Would she get the chance to meet her? Did this make a difference to their plans?

When she got back, Anna told Stephen what Mrs Lennox had said, without mentioning her own feelings. What she did say was, 'It'll be interesting to meet her.'

'You don't think she wants to move back into Dolphin Cottage, do you?' Stephen said in a worried voice. 'Oh God! This house-buying business is complicated!'

They sat drinking coffee in silence. Down in the harbour they saw Tristan arrive and with him was a tall woman with short, dark hair. She was wearing shorts and looking completely at home. Anna and Stephen watched them both get on board Wave Dancer and Jill, if it was her, helped get everyone else on board for the trip. There was no Gary today, only Tristan and Jill. Anna looked through the binoculars at them; Tristan said something to the woman, who laughed happily. He didn't look up at the cottage as he usually did.

Luckily, Anna had already arranged to go and look around the main county hospital that morning so she didn't have time to think about things too much. She drove there with Stephen who was going to visit the public library in the town to find out what he could about advertising companies in the area. Anna liked the hospital; it was the medical centre for the whole region so they saw a wide range of patients and problems. They told her they were usually short of nurses so she'd be welcome to apply for a job. But she might have to wait some time before she got a job at the same level as her one in London.

When they got back, they found a note on the kitchen table from Tristan.

Sorry to miss you. If you're back in time, we'll be in the Fisherman's from 5.

Tristan

'Mmm, we'll be in the Fisherman's. Interesting. Let's go,' said Stephen. 'We'd better find out if we're still buying the cottage.'

Anna quickly changed into her jeans and they went off to the pub. As they reached it, she saw Tristan and Jill sitting close together and chatting happily. Stephen took hold of Anna's hand as they went over. 'Hi, Tristan. We got your note. Here we are.'

They sat down at the same table and ordered coffee. Jill was introduced and she started talking about Dolphin Cottage. 'You've got the best view in the whole of Polreath from there, haven't you? I used to sit in the front garden watching everything in the harbour.'

'So do we,' said Anna. She tried hard not to stare at the attractive woman sitting opposite her.

'It's a lovely old place. Does the cold tap in the bathroom still make a funny noise when you turn it on? It used to drive me mad, but the owner never came to fix it.' And she gave Tristan a kiss.

Stephen said, 'I've mended it. It doesn't make a noise now.' Everybody seemed to be looking at everyone else – Jill at Tristan, Tristan at Anna, Anna and Stephen at Jill.

'Oh well, that's good,' she laughed. 'You sound the perfect people to buy it.'

Anna smiled at Stephen and thought, 'So he's told her, and it doesn't sound as if she's planning to move back in. Good, that's one thing less to worry about.'

'I've been in touch with my lawyer,' said Tristan. 'There

doesn't seem to be a problem. He's going to get things started. He needs the name of your lawyer, by the way. But we can do all that tomorrow, can't we?'

'Fine,' said Stephen. 'Anyone want another coffee?'

'Me, please,' said Anna, and Stephen went over to the bar. 'Did you have a good trip this morning?' Anna asked Tristan. 'We saw you both going out.'

And Jill answered, 'Yes, it was great. Just like old times, wasn't it?'

'Mm, yes. And you still can't tie a boat up properly,' Tristan smiled at her.

When Stephen came back with Anna's coffee, Tristan said,

'Come on Jill. We'd better go. We're going over to St Leven for the evening.'

A drive in the 'fishy' car and dinner at Gino's I bet, thought Anna, and felt terrible. Why did he say that? He didn't need to tell us where they were going. What's he doing? Is he trying to make me jealous?

'I'll come round tomorrow mid-morning, if that's all right,' Tristan continued. 'I'm glad everything seems to be working out well – with the cottage and everything.'

Later that night, for the first time in a long time, Anna turned away from Stephen when he wanted to make love.

Chapter 14 *Anna's last trip*

Friday was even hotter. There was no wind, not even a breeze, and the air was still. Stephen and Anna had a swim before breakfast, then stood in their front garden with their coffee, looking around them. They were both thinking that this view was going to be theirs – for ever, if they wanted. There would be days in the future when everything looked as calm and beautiful as today, and other times, in the winter, when storms would hit and the sea would become frightening.

Tristan came round at eleven. Anna was out walking. She and Stephen had already decided that she would go back to London by train that weekend to start work again on Monday morning – but Stephen would stay on another week to sort some things out with Tristan.

'You're not having second thoughts about selling the cottage, are you?' asked Stephen.

'No, not really. It's a big step, though, selling a family house, isn't it?' Tristan drank his coffee thoughtfully. 'But what about you two? Are you OK about it all? It's an even bigger step for you – a complete change of life, really.'

'I personally can't wait to say goodbye to the big city world of advertising,' said Stephen. 'I don't know how I've managed to do it for so long.'

Anna came back in to the cottage looking hot.

'I think I need another swim to cool down. There's no wind today.'

'Mm, I hate to say it but I think the weather is going to change,' said Tristan. 'The forecast says that there'll be a thunderstorm tonight.'

'Just at the right moment, at the end of our holiday!' laughed Anna. 'Perhaps it's trying to tell us something.'

'What,' said Stephen with a smile, 'like there'll be stormy times ahead in our lives?'

'Yeah. Just like in the movies,' Anna said. 'A good storm is the director's way of telling the audience that something terrible is going to happen.'

'Well, I'm going fishing this afternoon before the weather changes,' said Tristan. 'Anyone want to come?' But he was thinking, not anyone, just Anna . . . please.

'I won't,' replied Stephen. 'I want to make some phone calls to the office to see what the latest news is. You go Anna. It might be cooler on the water – and it'll be your last chance before you go back.'

At three that afternoon, Anna and Tristan left the harbour and went in the direction of the western rocks. Anna was happy that Stephen had suggested she came with Tristan. She wanted to be alone with him and think things through before she went back to London. The sea was flat and calm as they fished near the rocks.

'Did you have a good time last night at Gino's?' asked Anna. It was no good, she had to know. She was furious with herself, but she realised that she was jealous.

'We didn't go to Gino's, but yes, thanks, we had a nice evening,' he said.

Anna looked at him and found him looking at her.

'Jill went back this morning, to London,' said Tristan. 'She came to say goodbye. She's got a job in Singapore, starting next month.'

'Oh. How do you feel about that?' she asked.

'A bit sad, in some ways. But we'd already accepted that we had no future together, so it wasn't a big surprise. I'll miss her, though.'

Anna felt good. She had been a little bit jealous of Jill. She took Tristan's hand and said, 'I thought she was nice – and you two seemed to get on really well together. I thought she might be coming back to live here.'

Tristan pulled her close. 'Would you have liked that?'

'No, I'm sorry to say, I wouldn't.'

All her mixed-up feelings of the last couple of days were near the surface now. They began kissing. Neither of them wanted to stop. They lay on the floor of the boat, pulling off each other's clothes, and made love eagerly. All the things that they'd been holding back, trying to forget, were set free. Being responsible, being strong-minded, Stephen, Jill, everything – it was all gone from their minds. It was wonderful – a powerful and completely selfish act.

After lying there next to each other for a while, Anna turned over to face him. 'Oh hell! What have we done?'

'Changed the rules of the game a bit, I'm afraid,' replied Tristan kissing her gently, and feeling very loving towards her.

'I think it was my fault. I'm embarrassed to say it. I was jealous, seeing you with Jill,' Anna admitted.

'I was going to say "Now you know how *I* feel when you're with Stephen", but it's not the same. I surprise myself sometimes. I don't actually feel jealous of Stephen.

71

Funny, isn't it? But we didn't make love just because of Jill, did we?' he asked anxiously.

'No,' replied Anna, with a smile. 'Because of us.'

Tristan slowly got up, looked around to make sure nobody was near, and jumped over the side of the boat. 'Brrrr, that's fresh!' he said, shaking the water from his hair. 'Why don't you come in?' he said to Anna who was still sitting on the floor of the boat, looking over the side at him. She got into the water and swam with Tristan. The water was cold and took the heat from her body. Tristan climbed back into the boat and watched Anna as she swam towards him. 'You're beautiful, you know,' he said as he pulled her on board. Their cold bodies touched.

'Here.' Tristan passed her a towel from his bag.

They dried quickly and put their clothes on. 'Now what?' he said, but was afraid to hear her answer.

'Stephen must never know,' said Anna. 'We must never do that again. We can't! There's no way we can have an affair. Can you imagine, in a place this size – everyone would know about it. In fact, some bird probably saw us and is already spreading the news – to Mrs Lennox, no doubt!'

'Do you really think you can just switch off all your feelings, just like a tap? I'm not sure I can.'

'Well, we've got to.' Reality was hitting Anna, and she was beginning to worry. Had they ruined everything? Would she be able to hide it from Stephen? Should she tell him and make him come back to London and forget about buying the cottage? Tonight was the last night of their holidays, it would be natural for them to make love – could she do it?

'Anna, listen. I know the situation as well as you do. You're probably thinking it's not going to work, the three of us living in such a small place, and you may be right.' Tristan started the engine. He was feeling very confused. He didn't want this to be the only time that they made love. But he knew the next move was Anna's. So he continued. 'You've got a choice. Go back to London and take Stephen with you and forget all about Polreath and living here. Or leave things as they are and see what happens. You're going back to London tomorrow anyway. We won't see each other again until you come back. Maybe a bit of time and distance will help. I don't want to ruin everything for you – or for me, either. But I want you in my life.'

'Sounds simple, doesn't it?' said Anna. Tristan had his arm round Anna's waist. But now she moved gently away. 'You're right, though. When we get back, I think it'd be better if we just said goodbye for now. It'll be less complicated if all I have to do is think about behaving normally until I get on the train tomorrow.'

As the boat came into the harbour, Anna looked up at the cottage and waved to Stephen sitting in the front.

'Anna,' said Tristan quietly. 'I'm not sorry about what happened this afternoon, are you?'

'No. But I want to shut it away in a box, and not let it escape. Please, Tristan, can we try and pretend nothing has happened.'

Tristan kissed her. 'Bye, Anna,' he said sadly. 'I don't know how it'll be when we see each other again. But I'm glad you came to Polreath this summer.' He got into his car and drove off leaving Anna to walk home alone.

Chapter 15 *A stormy night*

'No fish?' said Stephen.

'Tristan had them all,' said Anna, and thought, that was the first lie. 'I thought we'd probably want to eat at Philpots tonight. Shall we?'

'Sure. We can celebrate the beginning of our new lives,' said Stephen.

'I'll go and book. It's Friday and they might be busy tonight.' Anna wanted to get out of the house. She booked a table for eight o'clock and then went into the shop. If Mrs Lennox had somehow managed to learn anything about her and Tristan she wanted to give her the chance to say it directly to her face. But fortunately nothing was said. When she got back, Stephen was waiting for her.

'You rushed out so quickly you didn't give me time to tell you my news!' he said, smiling happily. 'I rang Charlie to ask him about the chances of my having to leave the new company. He thought I was worried and tried to say nice things. But when I told him I wanted to leave, he laughed.'

'Why?' asked Anna.

'Because apparently the new managing director was just about to tell me that I had lost my job, and he was not looking forward to saying it,' said Stephen.

'When will this happen?'

'In a couple of months!' Stephen replied happily. 'I'll be free of Jardine's – and I'll have a "thank you and goodbye" present of a year's salary. Not bad, eh? Somebody, somewhere is taking care of us, don't you think? This is exactly what I wanted.'

'Stephen, that's great – if it's really what you want.'

'It is. Anna, are you having second thoughts?'

'No, not at all,' she replied quickly.

Stephen took hold of her as she walked past his chair on the way upstairs. She fell backwards onto him and he kissed the back of her neck.

'Mmm . . . salt and fish! You smell wonderful!'

'I need a shower.' She got up and kissed him on the nose.

The shower helped. 'Everything's working out well for him,' she thought. 'There's no way I can suddenly change my mind about living here. God, I feel awful. He would be so hurt if he ever found out. I'm a fool! I'm confused! I don't know what to think anymore.' She dried herself roughly. The main thing now was to get through the next few hours without a disaster. *Real* thinking would come later. She found Stephen in the front garden.

'Better?' he said.

'Yes, much.'

'Something's changed,' he said looking around.

'What do you mean?' she asked quickly.

'The air smells different. I think there is going to be a storm, after all.'

'Good,' she said before realising what she was saying.

As they went up the hill to Philpots they could hear thunder in the distance and the first whisper of wind cooled their faces. Over dinner, Stephen was full of plans – what he was going to do, when they'd be able to come back down, how they'd have to buy another car – or maybe he'd get a motorbike. Anna listened, smiled and said very little.

Their dinner was excellent and the wine helped Anna to relax more. When they left the restaurant, the wind had got stronger and big drops of rain were hitting the ground, hard. The storm was coming in from the west. Skellig was suddenly lit up by a flash of lightning. Stephen put his sweater over his head and they both ran down the street. Then they saw Tristan.

'Oh, hi!' said Tristan. 'I was just going to make sure the boat was tied up properly.' Another flash of lightning showed the white tops of the waves in the harbour.

'Want some help?' asked Stephen, but Tristan was already moving away. The air was electric.

'Come on, Stephen,' said Anna running down the street. 'Let's get home before it gets any worse.'

As they reached the cottage, there was a huge crash of thunder. They stood in the doorway and watched. With each flash of lightning, the sky was lit up and they could see ghostly figures in the harbour, checking boat ropes.

'The water's high tonight,' said Stephen. 'We've never seen it so high – no wonder Tristan was worried.'

Stephen and Anna went upstairs to bed. But the storm was so wild and beautiful. Anna stood at the bedroom window with Stephen behind her, his arms holding her close.

'Next week'll be strange without you here,' he said.

'No, it won't. You'll be so busy arranging things you won't have time to notice. In any case, it'll give you a chance to get used to it,' replied Anna.

'In what way?'

'Well, I might not be able to move down here as soon as you. I don't know about my job and things yet, do I? You might have to spend a bit of time here alone,' said Anna, and added quickly, 'before I can join you.'

'Oh. We'll have to talk about that next weekend. I don't want to come back without you. I want to start this together,' and he kissed the back of her neck.

They went to bed and reached for each other. His body was usually so familiar and lovely but tonight she felt uncomfortable with his body beside her and her dreams that night were full of disturbing pictures.

In the morning, it took a long time to wake from her deep sleep – the dreams were still pulling her back down. Stephen wasn't there, so she slowly got out of bed and walked to the window. The scene outside was much changed. The storm had passed but the sky was grey. Rain had washed away all the summer's dirt and the streets looked fresh. She looked down at the harbour – Wave Dancer was still there, good – but she noticed three other boats on the beach, on their sides. Several people were down there, standing around, including Stephen and Tristan. She turned away from the window.

When Stephen came back, she was ready to leave. She walked around the cottage saying goodbye to it, wondering when – and if – she'd return. Her feelings this morning matched the sky. Stephen thought she was unhappy because she was going back to London, and she let him think that.

They said a rather sad goodbye at Kingham station. She stood at the carriage window, waving to Stephen until he disappeared. Then she suddenly started to cry.

Chapter 16 *The end of the affair*

Back in London, Anna tried to get herself back into her normal routine. She was busy at the hospital, and that kept her mind fully occupied. Everybody kept telling her how well she looked, and younger, too, and that the seaside was obviously good for her.

The routine of her familiar life helped her to calm down. In the evenings, in the flat alone, she thought about Polreath and Tristan and Stephen, and she gradually began to realise that what had happened was no more than a holiday love affair. A mixture of lots of different things had let it happen – Stephen's work crisis, her need for some sort of change, the fact that Tristan was very attractive and was attracted to her, and the fact that he was so open and easy to talk to – unlike Stephen recently – and of course the magic of the sun and the sea.

But understanding it didn't make her feel any better. She felt guilty that she had started something with Tristan that she knew now she couldn't continue. She had a horrible feeling, however, that it was different for Tristan – but then he wasn't married; he had less to lose.

And she was right. Tristan couldn't get Anna out of his mind. The only time he felt calm was when he went out fishing. And as for talking to Stephen – well, it was getting more and more difficult.

Stephen, however, wanted to get on with the business of

buying Dolphin Cottage. They had agreed on the sale price, and he wanted to pay Tristan the deposit before he went back to London at the weekend. So early on Wednesday morning he went down to the harbour and found Tristan busy on his boat.

'Morning, Tristan,' he said. 'Didn't see you yesterday. Everything OK?'

'Yes, fine thanks,' Tristan replied as he untied the ropes that held Wave Dancer to the harbour wall. 'I'm just going to pick up the lobster pots I put down yesterday, behind Skellig.'

'Right. Look, can we meet tomorrow evening? I should have the cheque by then,' said Stephen.

'In the Fisherman's about seven?' said Tristan turning Wave Dancer away from the harbour wall. 'Sorry, Stephen, can't stop to talk now, I've got a lot to do.'

On Thursday morning, Anna woke up with a clear head – as soon as she opened her eyes she knew that they couldn't buy Dolphin Cottage. They couldn't live in Polreath. She knew that seeing Tristan every day would be a constant reminder and, if she was honest, she was afraid that what had happened once could happen again. Was she really strong enough to cut the relationship? Tristan was lovely – too lovely to hurt any more. Surely it was better to end it all now while she still had the choice. Stephen need never know.

Anna stood in the shower, letting the water run over her face. 'Oh Stephen, I'm sorry. You'd never trust me again if you found out, would you?' Anna thought. She realised she didn't want to lose him and the life they had together. True, some of the early excitement had disappeared over the ten years of their married life, and he could be difficult to live with but she knew him so well. She knew what he liked to eat, she knew the way he combed his hair, she knew what he would think about a programme on TV. He was part of her.

The first thing she had to do was stop Stephen buying Dolphin Cottage tonight. He was going to be very confused about why she had changed her mind and horribly disappointed. And he'd have to find a new job somewhere. Oh God! How was she going to explain her reasons – maybe she could introduce the idea of moving out of London but not going quite so far as Cornwall. It was true she had been thinking about the things she would miss when they moved – her friends, the fun of living in the capital city. What about Brighton! Lots of London people moved to Brighton, and she and Stephen had always enjoyed the weekends they had spent there.

Just as she was walking through to the kitchen, the phone rang. It made her jump. 'Stephen, or Mum,' she thought. 'They're the only people who'd phone so early in the morning. Or maybe it's Tristan.' Whoever it was, she wasn't ready to speak. She picked it up nervously.

It was Stephen. 'Anna, I've just seen Tristan. He's just told me something. We've got to talk.'

Anna's heart froze.